SUMMARY

Of

MINDSET

The New Psychology of Success

Carol Dweck

Sir. Summary

TABLE OF CONTENTS

INTRODUCTION

Mindset: The New Psychology of Success is a book by Carol S. Dweck about human thoughts, and how these thoughts can greatly influence the way we live our everyday lives. This book is written in the form of a self-help book, so readers will find many interesting and educational tidbits of advice on how to live the best life possible.

What is really interesting and worth admiring about this book is that Dweck did a tremendous amount of work before she wrote her book. Based on many observations during many years of research, the author developed something called a "mindset" of how different humans perceive different things in different ways and thus live differently. The author recognized that, based on her observations, there are two distinct, radically different mindsets; however, both of these separate mindsets can be connected with some success.

Truly interesting literature to read and to study, *Mindset: The New Psychology Today* is a book that is here to open new horizons. The book itself is never boring or dull. On the contrary, it will take a reader on a journey that will teach him something new and valuable to lead him toward a better life.

SUMMARY

PART 1:
TWO DIFFERENT MINDSETS

The first part of the book and its first chapter opens with the author's thesis that working with children can greatly help us in learning and developing our innate qualities and thus learning how to understand the differences between people. While observing children, we can see from an early age how they are different from each other and how each child has different behavior.

Here the author continues and says that when we observe children from a young age, we see that children have developed distinctive behavior from dealing with specific life experiences. Here the author says that while some children see their failures as clear proofs of their inability or incapability, other children see these failures as something else. They perceive failures as challenges, something that will eventually lead them toward improvement because they will eventually learn something new. The second group learns that failure is not as bad as it may seem at the time.

Later the author tries to explain what the secret is that allows people to properly handle failures. The thing is that these people know that, in order to achieve something or to succeed in something, it takes effort and hard work. Only this hard work will enable someone to reach something that he or she intends to achieve. If a person is smart, that is of course a good thing, but that person can become even smarter and thus can learn new things that can help in life. If a failure occurs, it is only a bridge toward new learning, new lessons and new improvements that will eventually lead to a better life.

But this is something good, because people are indeed intended to work, and yes, to fail, in order to grow. If not, we will stagnate, being limited with our own obstacles that we did not want to deal with.

PART 2:
ARE STRENGTHS AND WEAKNESSES INNATE? UNDERSTANDING THE POTENTIAL

For a long period of time many scientists believed that these two human traits were innate and thus something that could not be changed in any way. But the newest studies show that these two different traits are separate and that they need to be perceived as separate – the presence of one does not necessarily mean the absence of the other.

What about the IQ test developed by Alfred Binet? Is his IQ test something that can be considered as the only strong measurement of a person's intelligence and a person's intellectual abilities? The answer to that is something that Binet said many times: every human being can improve his or her own intellectual abilities by practice and with training. But what is most important is that intelligence (which can be improved) combined with effort and purpose lead to success in any field of life. This is something that will help a person to be "different." Here difference refers to not being part of the crowd of people who live their lives unaware of their purposes and their life's meaning.

What about understanding a person's potential? How do these two groups of people see and understand their own potential?

When the author talks about understanding a person's potential, it is important to emphasize here that people with fixed mindsets perceive success and everything connected to it very differently than people with growth mindsets. Here the author says that people with fixed mindsets believe that they must constantly prove that they fit in a certain pattern or "image" of some sort. People with growth mindsets believe that regardless of their strengths and weaknesses, they can still grow and learn if appropriate training combined with learning and dedication is applied.

Examples for this can be seen everywhere in the world. For example, many people that are now successful or famous were once just ordinary people like many of us. Many of these now-successful people also faced failures and rejections or got dumped by their boyfriends/girlfriends, but that did not stop them from moving forward, towards success and slowly but surely advancing towards their goals. They did not try to hide their weaknesses and shortcomings. Instead they worked on resolving and conquering their flaws, because that is the only path to true success.

Contrary to that, people with fixed mindset can be overwhelmed with feelings that they are not worthy enough, lack of self-esteem, and even blame life circumstances for not giving them enough chances for success. This of course will not and cannot lead to true success, not because people with fixed a mindset cannot succeed, but because their way of thinking and living does not allow them to reach success.

People with fixed mindsets often blow things out of proportion, such as when they experience some kind of failure they exaggerate, but do not want to take any risks or make any effort, two very important ingredients for success. People with a growth mindset always try to look at their failure (or defeat in certain areas of their life) as a valuable lesson that will help them to be smarter and to work even harder in the future.

There is a big gap between success and failure. The reason for that is because of how we choose to act upon failure and how we are trying to reach success.

PART 3:
WE WANT TO BE UNIQUE IN EVERYTHING

Humans are designed to be unique. This, however, does not refer to our physical appearance, our racial distinctions or other things like that. Each and every one of us is created or born (or whatever you see fit) differently. We have different abilities and different potentials, and different choices are given to us with different outcomes possible. And that is something astounding and great about our lives. But what is not so great is when we think that we can achieve goals without investing our effort. That is what leads to many disappointments and failures and causes many people to give up.

Here is where difference between fixed and growth mindsets also takes part. A growth mindset says that if I want to have a certain ability or skill or if I want to know something, I need to invest my time into learning that particular skill or piece of knowledge. It just does not work any other way. People are born with certain gifts and that is true, but only training and learning ensures excellence and progress.

When it comes to validations and approvals of the world regarding our own success and excellence there are also difference between these two mindsets. People with fixed mindsets will very often seek approval from others. This means that they will want others to say to them how good they are in something that they do. People with growth mindsets do not do that, not because they do not care what others think about their success, but because they do not require other people's reactions for their success to be possible.

This can greatly impact our world and how we perceive it and this is why it is important for us to be able to differentiate between growth and fixed mindsets.

PART 4:
LEARNING IS THE KEY FOR SUCCESS

The author continues and states that we live in a world which is divided between people who learn and are open to learning, and people who do not wish to learn. The latter group of people strongly (and sadly) believes that the world is a place where everyone gets something according to their own sets of gifts.

Why do people with fixed mindsets fear challenge? Is it because they cannot win? Well, in a manner of speaking yes, but it is not because they truly *cannot* win. It is because they are afraid that if they do not succeed their entire perception of themselves will be endangered in some way. And this is precisely why people with fixed mindsets, contrary to people with growth mindsets, are so very often limited in their lives. This happens in every segment of life which requires learning and faces challenges along the way.

The same thing is true about relationships between people and the author is not talking only about romantic relationships, even though the greatest emphasis is on that particular type of relationships. Who we date is something that every person chooses for him or herself and that decision is based on many different factors, which in the end, influence their decisions. For example, some people choose a partner that will "worship" them and put them on a pedestal. Other people choose a partner who will enable them to grow. A problem occurs when two different mindsets enter a relationship, because they perceive everything differently. What can, for one person, be a challenge worthy of trying and thus learning, is for another person an obstacle that can seem taller than Mount Everest.

The author does not say that a relationship between two different mindsets is not possible, but if people want their relationship to succeed, effort and compromise from both sides will be needed.

What about business life and relationships between CEOs and their subordinates? What about CEOs with fixed mindsets?

Well, if you have a boss, with a fixed mindset, he or she will almost always dismiss criticism directed towards him or her. By criticism I mean constructive criticism, the kind that is aimed toward giving new ideas and possibly improving the old ones. A CEO with a fixed mindset will often think that his ideas about how a business is run is just the way it has to be and that there is absolutely no need or room for improvements. On the other hand, a CEO with a growth mindset will always search for improvement and will welcome criticism.

PART 5:
GROWTH INSPIRES GROWTH
IN OTHERS AS WELL

When we see people with growth mindsets, we do not need evidence of some sort that these people have growth a mindset. We see that they have a growth mindset. We somehow feel that. These people inspire other people and when other people see and work with people with growth mindsets, their own abilities and wishes for improvement and learning gets boosted to a higher level.

When we see people with fixed mindsets, we will see that those people almost always choose their safe zone. Why is that? Because in their safe zone, they are- safe and nothing can surprise them (and prompt them to action, which possibly requires taking risk, failing and learning something new) or put them out where risk "lurks."

Risk is something that people with fixed mindset are trying to avoid as much as possible. But people with a growth mindset know that risk – together with small steps and patience – is something that is not only important, but also vital, for success. For example, if a person wants to learn how to be good in romantic relationships and how to find a partner that will suit him or her perfectly, that person needs to devote herself to learning and needs to be patient. Because if your previous relationship was bad and you made some mistakes, that does not mean that your future relationship will be the same. I mean, it can be, but that will only suggest that you have not learned anything from your past mistakes. But if you look closely at your previous relationships and you detect your mistakes and decide that you will work on them so that they do not happen in the future (or at least minimize their re-occurrence), success will come. It will require time and effort, but success will eventually come. That is why thoughts like, "I suck at relationships, women do not love me," because of your past relationships are simply a wrong way of perceiving things. This type of mistake is precisely where the secret between fixed and growth mindsets lies.

Here is one of the most common traits that each person with a fixed mindset desires: a strong desire to be loved, to be special and to be superior to others. Here lies the main reason why so many people think that being just a normal, ordinary person is insufficient in this world and why so many people thrive to be as superior as possible.

Of course, we often end up achieving that superiority in a wrong and superficial way.

Also, many people with fixed mindsets somehow feel that they are entitled to abuse others, especially when fixed-mindset people gain power or influence. We see that every day – in politics, economy, educational systems, business, even in our most intimate relationships. Fixed-mindset people abuse, are condescending, have no shame and instead of being modest they always try to emphasize (or over-emphasize) their importance through their success.

In contrast, people with growth mindsets remain humble and do not wish to stand out from others. They do that not because they cannot, but because they are perfectly aware of their success and their strengths and thus they do not require some outside input that will tell them how great they are. That is why people with growth mindsets do not allow their failures to determine their ways. If we want to grow, we will accept the fact that if we try something and especially if we are not good at that (that happens more often if we are newbies in doing something), we will sometimes fail. We will fall and sometimes suffer a defeat. And sure, a defeat is always a defeat and they are not easy to cope with this, but a defeat (or defeats) must no stop us from achieving our goals.

Defeats and failures are excellent ways for us to learn something, because if we analyze why we failed, we will learn the reason and if we try that same challenge later, our result will surely be different in a better way. Defeat and failure can (and often serve to) motivate us. When, through that motivation, we finally achieve our goal and succeed, we will find that success to be a lot sweeter and we will enjoy it a lot more.

PART 6:
ABILITIES VERSUS ACCOMPLISHMENTS

There are a lot of people who perceive successful people as people who were successful immediately from the start and who just waited for the right moment for their brilliance to come out, but that is not true. It is not enough to be a genius to be successful. It takes a lot more than that.

There are many examples in human history where we see that it takes a lot more than just plain human genius for someone to be successful. Yes, there were some people who preferred working alone and thus achieving their success, but most of them became successful with time and by working with other people that were similar to them.

Hard work is crucial for success, but it is true that some people are born gifted. What the author deduced during her research is that gifted people love challenge and their work is almost an ideal combination of ability and mindset. Although being gifted means that a person can achieve success in a field where that person is gifted faster than people who are not gifted, it certainly does not mean that gifted people can succeed without hard work, investing effort and dedication.

What happens to our minds when we change or when we are changing our mindsets to growth mindsets?

Well, exactly that happens – our minds change. Our perspectives change. We start to see the world and its opportunities in different ways than we used to.

Let's look at the educational system.

If we have teachers and professors with growth mindsets, we will see that these people are teaching children differently than teachers with fixed mindsets. Fixed-mindset teachers will perceive students as being either dumb or smart. For example, if you can learn something fast, you are smart, but if you cannot, then you are dumb. That kind of perspective damages not just students (by influencing their self-esteem for example), but it also damages the overall educational system. On the other hand, teachers with growth mindsets always try to develop a sense of confidence and thus they try to raise the self-esteem in students. Instead of thinking and saying, "You cannot learn as fast as they can because you are dumb," their perspective is a lot more open, self-confidence-boosting and supporting.

When the author talks about skills and abilities, she clearly states that every skill and ability has some learning components. The same thing goes for anything, even for art. While a gifted artist will surely make better paintings, he still requires a lot of practice for his gift to be used the best way possible.

Every skill and/or ability can be learned. That closely depends on several factors. One of them is whether a person is gifted or not. But regardless of that, with time, practice and dedication most skills and abilities that a person wants to master can indeed be mastered.

PART 7:
HOW A WINNER THINKS DETERMINES HIS TRIUMPHS AND DEFEATS

Sports is another part of life where many people strongly believe that talent is something that is more than sufficient for someone to succeed and to become a top athlete. But that is also something that is not true and that point of view comes from fixed mindsets. A growth mindset suggests that even here success comes through hard work and practice, and the evidence for that is all around us.

In sports, a person can become a victim of his or her own talent. This mostly happens because talented people can often neglect the necessity and benefits of hard work, while at the same time over-emphasizing their talent. This is where a person's personality comes on the scene and this is where we can yet again see the difference in perception between fixed and growth mindsets. Fixed mindsets will over-emphasize the element of talent, while growth mindsets will know that talent cannot be fully used without training.

But the term "champion" or a "winner" does not necessarily have to be a term that is used in sports. That term is also used in everyday life. Normal people who take their challenges and conquer them are also winners. Winning does not necessarily have to mean earning a gold medal.

Being a winner means succeeding in learning and thus surpassing your own limits. This is exactly what can give people that extra boost to continue. Mistakes that will happen and that are sometimes unavoidable serve as a wake-up call.

PART 8:
GROWING IN BUSINESS AND IN RELATIONSHIPS

Business is another part of life where recognizing the difference between a fixed and a growth mindset is very important. Here the author states that it is possible for most leaders to have a growth mindset instead of a fixed one, and that nurturing and developing a growth mindset is something that is very important.

Fixed mindsets behave in a way that tells others that they are the best, they are luckier and smarter than others, that they have achieved their success in a unique way, and that because of that they are better than people who are less successful than they are. Moreover, fixed mindsets are so focused on the greatness of success that they cannot perceive failure as something possible and real. Growth mindsets operate differently. They also cherish their success and they are aware of it, but they also know how they achieved that success. Growth mindsets know that for them to succeed they need to invest effort and that failures that may happen are just another way of learning something.

When the author talks about relationships, she speaks also of different perceptions on breakups and relationships in general. While fixed mindsets perceive a breakup as evidence of failure in that person, growth mindsets perceive breakups as a chance of learning something. Also, people with fixed mindsets see a successful relationship as flawless compatibility, while growth mindsets knows that there will be times in any relationship where problems will occur and that not everything is "sunshine and rainbows," but that that is perfectly normal.

There are many areas where we can see differences in perceptions between these two mindsets. Growth mindsets also see a partner's flaws as something that can be improved.

What is important is that mindset, regardless of which area of life we are talking about, can be changed. But for that, in addition to strong will, it takes continued effort combined with patience to move forward, even when it seems that things are not getting any better.

ANALYSIS

Mindset: The New Psychology Today is a great book about human mindsets and how we behave, think and live. At the core of the book are two different mindsets: fixed (oriented towards fixed traits and facts about life, and the idea that a person's abilities cannot be changed) and a growth or learned mindset (oriented towards learning, slow but thorough and possible progression towards success).

What I liked about this book the most is how the author explained many segments of our life from the perspective of these two mindsets. The author, in addition to giving explanations of how these mindsets function, always encourages her readers by saying that it is possible to achieve the goals that we want to achieve. We can see that the book is written by a person who dedicated a lot of her time to studying how we work. This research not only enriches the book with useful information but it also helps the book to be a great guidebook for people who want positive change in their life. The book is never boring and even though it is written in a scientific way it is easy-to-read and its practical use makes it one great read.

QUIZ

You want to know more? If your answer is 'yes' then this quiz is just right for you. Questions are simple and answers can be found in the summary section.

QUESTION 1

Which are two mindsets that this book is about?

    a) Fixed and opened.

    b) Growth and slow.

    c) Fixed and growth.

    d) Slow and fast mindset.

QUESTION 2

"People with fixed mindsets see successful people as people who achieved their success through hard work and learning."

TRUE   FALSE

QUESTION 3

"The answer on that is something that also _____ told many times and that is that every human being _____ its own intellectual abilities by _____ and with _____."

QUESTION 4

What is a trait of a mindset opposite of fixed one?

   a) Being better and greater than other.

   b) Being able to win in everything that you do.

   c) Knowing that talent and great ability is something that is innate.

   d) Knowing that with time and through effort many things can be learned and mastered.

QUESTION 5

"Being a winner means to succeed in learning and thus surpassing your own limits."

TRUE   FALSE

QUIZ ANSWERS

QUESTION 1 – c

QUESTION 2 – FALSE

QUESTION 3 – 'Binet, can improve, practices, training.'

QUESTION 4 – d

QUESTION 5 – TRUE

CONCLUSION

Mindset: The New Psychology of Success is a book that amazed me. This was not because the book contained some universal recipe for how to become successful in five easy steps. Sure, if you read the book (and I strongly suggest that you do) you will find a lot of practical advice on how to improve your own productivity and how to become more successful, but that is not all this book has to offer.

First of all, the book came from an author who spent many years studying and researching human behavior, and after that, decided to put everything she learned into this book. And this is how *Mindset: The New Psychology Today* was born. It does not contain some dark and mysterious secrets of the human mind. Instead, the book contains descriptions of two human mindsets – the fixed mindset and the growth mindset – and explanations of how these two mindsets function in our everyday lives. Everything is explained in a clear and very easy-to-understand way, which is another great thing, because it means that many readers will be able to read the book and to understand it perfectly. The book is so interesting – I read it in no time, even though it was written by a scientist! This is definitely one of those books that are very easy to understand and to apply its message to our everyday lives.

Mindset: The New Psychology Today is a book that you need to read. It will open your eyes and help you understand why things are the way they are, and that with time and effort many things can be changed. That applies to your life too!

Thank You, and more...

Thank you for spending your time to read this book, I hope now you hold a greater knowledge about **Mindset.**

There are like-minded individuals like you who would like to learn about **Mindset,** this information can be useful for them as well. So, I would highly appreciate if you post a good review on amazon kindle where you purchased this book. And to share it in your social media (Facebook, Instagram, etc.)

Not only does it help me make a living, but it helps others obtain this knowledge as well. So I would highly appreciate it!!

www.amazon.com

We have other shortened books available for you as well by EZ-reader:

1- Me Before You – Shortened version

http://www.amazon.com/Before-You-Shortened-Audiobook-Hardcover-ebook/dp/B01BUQLLX2/ref=sr_1_3?s=digital-text&ie=UTF8&qid=1457420168&sr=1-3&keywords=ez-reader

2- The Girl on the Train – Shortened version

http://www.amazon.com/Girl-Train-Hawkins-Shortened-Paperback-ebook/dp/B01CIURTXA/ref=sr_1_1?s=digital-text&ie=UTF8&qid=1457420168&sr=1-1&keywords=ez-reader

3- Good to Great – Shortened version

http://www.amazon.com/Good-Great-Shortened-Companies-Shortened---ebook/dp/B01CCN3A9O/ref=sr_1_2?s=digital-text&ie=UTF8&qid=1457420168&sr=1-2&keywords=ez-reader

4- To Kill a Mockingbird – Shortened version

http://www.amazon.com/Kill-Mockingbird-Shortened-Hardcover-Audiobook-ebook/dp/B01BMT4YJU/ref=sr_1_5?s=digital-text&ie=UTF8&qid=1457419885&sr=1-5&keywords=ez-reader

5- The Martian – Shortened version

http://www.amazon.com/Martian-Shortened-Paperback-Audiobook-Audible-ebook/dp/B01C02E1BE/ref=sr_1_4?s=digital-text&ie=UTF8&qid=1457420168&sr=1-4&keywords=ez-reader

For more books from EZ-READER, please visit:

http://www.amazon.com/s/ref=nb_sb_no
ss_1?url=search-alias=digital-text&field-
keywords=ez-
reader&rh=n%3A133140011,k%3Aez-
reader

Thank you for reading and your time, please give us a good review on amazon, so we can write more summaries for you!!

Made in the USA
Lexington, KY
15 June 2017